Books of Theo von Taane

book	ISBN / order nr.
Football Tacticboard & Training Workbook	9783734749605
Badminton Tacticboard & Training Workbook	9783734749643
Baseball Tacticboard & Training Workbook	9783734749650
Basketball Tacticboard & Training Workbook	9783734749681
Bowling Tacticboard & Training Workbook	9783734749698
Cricket Tacticboard & Training Workbook	9783734749711
Ice Hockey Tacticboard & Training Workbook	9783734749728
Fencing Tacticboard & Training Workbook	9783734749735
Field Hockey Tacticboard & Training Workbook	9783734749810
Football (Soccer) Tacticboard & Training Workbook	9783734749827
Futsal Tacticboard & Training Workbook	9783734749834
Handball Tacticboard & Training Workbook	9783734749841
Lacrosse Women Tacticboard & Training Workbook	9783734749858
Lacrosse Men Tacticboard & Training Workbook	9783734749865
Netball Tacticboard & Training Workbook	9783734749872
Rugby Tacticboard & Training Workbook	9783734749889
Chess Tacticboard & Training Workbook	9783734749896
Squash Tacticboard & Training Workbook	9783734749902
Tennis Tacticboard & Training Workbook	9783734749919
Table Tennis Tacticboard & Training Workbook	9783734749926
Volleyball Tacticboard & Training Workbook	9783734749933
Water Polo Tacticboard & Training Workbook	9783734749940

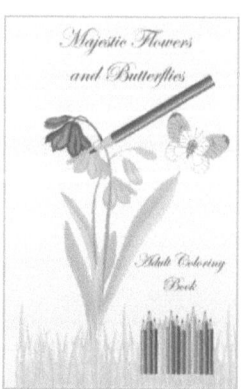

Majestic Flowers and Butterflies
- Adult Coloring Book - ISBN: 9783739227085

This coloring book for adults contains 36 beautiful patterns of various flowers. Experience hours full of stress relief, mindful calm, creative expression and fun.
Use crayons, felt-tip pens and colored pencils to give the patterns a personal touch.
Millions of people worldwide have rediscovered the simple relaxation and joy of coloring!
Join this community and find yourself enchanted by the magical passion of inspiring coloring.